Multiplication & Division Workbook (grades 3, 4, and 5)

Mr. Patterson

First printing edition 2019.

Table of Contents

3rd, 4th and 5th Grade Multiplication

How do we solve 1-digit multiplication problems?

First let's look at a visual explanation of how we group different numbers into each other!

$$2 \times 3 = 6$$

To understand how we solve for 2 x 3 we must first understand some of the word meanings.

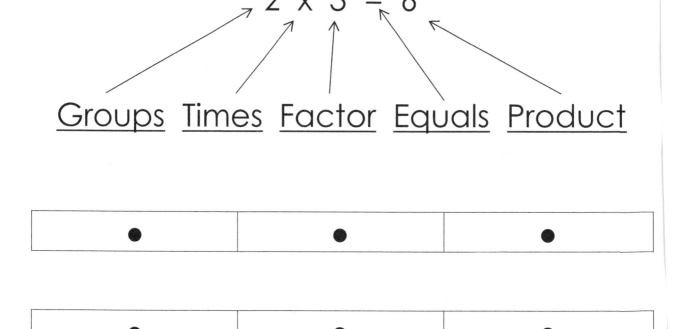

Notice how there is 2 rows (groups) and there are 3 dots (factor) for each row.

If we add all the dots up we get the same answer from before, 6!

Let's get started with practice questions to help you become a multiplication master!

*Note: All the answers to each problem can be found towards the end of the book in the <u>Answer Key</u> section.

Basic Multiplication (2x to 5x)

Name: _____ Date: _____

2 x 1 =	3 x 4 =	4 x 7 =
2 x 2 =	3 x 5 =	4 x 8 =
2 x 3 =	3 x 6 =	4 x 9 =
2 x 4 =	3 x 7 =	5 x 1 =
2 x 5 =	3 x 8 =	5 x 2 =
2 x 6 =	3 x 9 =	5 x 3 =
2 x 7 =	4 x 1 =	5 x 4 =
2 x 8 =	4 x 2 =	5 x 5 =
2 x 9=	4 x 3 =	5 x 6 =
3 x 1 =	4 x 4 =	5 x 7 =
3 x 2 =	4 x 5 =	5 x 8 =
3 x 3 =	4 x 6 =	5 x 9 =

Basic Multiplication (6x to 9x)

6 x 1 =	7 x 4 =	8 x 7 =
6 x 2 =	7 x 5 =	8 x 8 =
6 x 3 =	7 x 6 =	8 x 9 =
6 x 4 =	7 x 7 =	9 x 1 =
6 x 5 =	7 x 8 =	9 x 2 =
6 x 6 =	7 x 9 =	9 x 3 =
6 x 7 =	8 x 1 =	9 x 4 =
6 x 8 =	8 x 2 =	9 x 5 =
6 x 9 =	8 x 3 =	9 x 6 =
7 x 1 =	8 x 4 =	9 x 7 =
7 x 2 =	8 x 5 =	9 x 8 =
7 x 3 =	8 x 6 =	9 x 9 =

Basic Multiplication (1x-9x)

Name: _____ Date: _____

$$\begin{array}{r} 8 \\ \times\,6 \\ \hline \end{array} \qquad \begin{array}{r} 8 \\ \times\,9 \\ \hline \end{array} \qquad \begin{array}{r} 2 \\ \times\,8 \\ \hline \end{array} \qquad \begin{array}{r} 4 \\ \times\,6 \\ \hline \end{array} \qquad \begin{array}{r} 3 \\ \times\,8 \\ \hline \end{array}$$

$$\begin{array}{r} 3 \\ \times\,4 \\ \hline \end{array} \qquad \begin{array}{r} 5 \\ \times\,2 \\ \hline \end{array} \qquad \begin{array}{r} 6 \\ \times\,3 \\ \hline \end{array} \qquad \begin{array}{r} 6 \\ \times\,4 \\ \hline \end{array} \qquad \begin{array}{r} 8 \\ \times\,8 \\ \hline \end{array}$$

$$\begin{array}{r} 5 \\ \times\,6 \\ \hline \end{array} \qquad \begin{array}{r} 8 \\ \times\,5 \\ \hline \end{array} \qquad \begin{array}{r} 5 \\ \times\,1 \\ \hline \end{array} \qquad \begin{array}{r} 4 \\ \times\,2 \\ \hline \end{array} \qquad \begin{array}{r} 7 \\ \times\,9 \\ \hline \end{array}$$

$$\begin{array}{r} 3 \\ \times\,6 \\ \hline \end{array} \qquad \begin{array}{r} 9 \\ \times\,2 \\ \hline \end{array} \qquad \begin{array}{r} 3 \\ \times\,5 \\ \hline \end{array} \qquad \begin{array}{r} 2 \\ \times\,2 \\ \hline \end{array} \qquad \begin{array}{r} 6 \\ \times\,2 \\ \hline \end{array}$$

$$\begin{array}{r} 5 \\ \times\,7 \\ \hline \end{array} \qquad \begin{array}{r} 3 \\ \times\,7 \\ \hline \end{array} \qquad \begin{array}{r} 4 \\ \times\,4 \\ \hline \end{array} \qquad \begin{array}{r} 8 \\ \times\,7 \\ \hline \end{array} \qquad \begin{array}{r} 3 \\ \times\,3 \\ \hline \end{array}$$

Room for Solving

Basic Multiplication (1x-9x)

Name: _____ Date: _____

2 x 3	7 x 1	8 x 8	6 x 8	2 x 8
2 x 2	6 x 1	2 x 5	6 x 4	3 x 1
4 x 9	2 x 6	6 x 5	1 x 8	9 x 4
4 x 4	8 x 7	5 x 8	1 x 6	2 x 4
4 x 7	1 x 3	3 x 4	6 x 6	9 x 5

Room for Solving

Basic Multiplication (1x-9x)

Name: _____ Date: _____

10 x 2	10 x 4	7 x 10	3 x 10	2 x 1
3 x 9	1 x 8	8 x 6	4 x 8	1 x 2
3 x 7	10 x 8	9 x 2	9 x 10	8 x 10
6 x 10	4 x 3	4 x 6	10 x 6	3 x 5
1 x 7	9 x 1	1 x 5	1 x 10	2 x 5

Room for Solving

Basic Multiplication (1x-9x)

Name: _____ Date: _____

$$\begin{array}{r} 9 \\ \times\ 2 \\ \hline \end{array} \qquad \begin{array}{r} 7 \\ \times\ 2 \\ \hline \end{array} \qquad \begin{array}{r} 9 \\ \times\ 4 \\ \hline \end{array} \qquad \begin{array}{r} 3 \\ \times\ 3 \\ \hline \end{array} \qquad \begin{array}{r} 2 \\ \times\ 7 \\ \hline \end{array}$$

$$\begin{array}{r} 5 \\ \times\ 10 \\ \hline \end{array} \qquad \begin{array}{r} 10 \\ \times\ 8 \\ \hline \end{array} \qquad \begin{array}{r} 4 \\ \times\ 2 \\ \hline \end{array} \qquad \begin{array}{r} 7 \\ \times\ 4 \\ \hline \end{array} \qquad \begin{array}{r} 5 \\ \times\ 9 \\ \hline \end{array}$$

$$\begin{array}{r} 6 \\ \times\ 5 \\ \hline \end{array} \qquad \begin{array}{r} 6 \\ \times\ 2 \\ \hline \end{array} \qquad \begin{array}{r} 7 \\ \times\ 7 \\ \hline \end{array} \qquad \begin{array}{r} 8 \\ \times\ 3 \\ \hline \end{array} \qquad \begin{array}{r} 8 \\ \times\ 7 \\ \hline \end{array}$$

$$\begin{array}{r} 10 \\ \times\ 3 \\ \hline \end{array} \qquad \begin{array}{r} 5 \\ \times\ 5 \\ \hline \end{array} \qquad \begin{array}{r} 9 \\ \times\ 10 \\ \hline \end{array} \qquad \begin{array}{r} 2 \\ \times\ 5 \\ \hline \end{array} \qquad \begin{array}{r} 3 \\ \times\ 7 \\ \hline \end{array}$$

$$\begin{array}{r} 10 \\ \times\ 6 \\ \hline \end{array} \qquad \begin{array}{r} 4 \\ \times\ 6 \\ \hline \end{array} \qquad \begin{array}{r} 2 \\ \times\ 3 \\ \hline \end{array} \qquad \begin{array}{r} 5 \\ \times\ 4 \\ \hline \end{array} \qquad \begin{array}{r} 6 \\ \times\ 4 \\ \hline \end{array}$$

Room for
Solving

Basic Multiplication (1x-9x)

Name: _____ Date: _____

9 x 7	10 x 6	4 x 2	7 x 4	10 x 5
3 x 2	4 x 8	7 x 7	7 x 2	9 x 4
3 x 4	5 x 7	4 x 5	8 x 3	10 x 8
4 x 4	9 x 3	8 x 6	8 x 7	5 x 3
6 x 4	5 x 5	5 x 10	3 x 5	10 x 3

Room for Solving

Basic Multiplication (1x-9x)

Name: _____ Date: _____

5 x 6	5 x 8	10 x 1	9 x 1	2 x 1
1 x 9	7 x 4	6 x 8	9 x 2	5 x 10
7 x 7	5 x 7	8 x 5	1 x 8	10 x 10
3 x 6	1 x 2	3 x 3	3 x 10	4 x 8
5 x 0	5 x 9	6 x 10	4 x 4	9 x 8

Room for
Solving

2-digit x 1-digit Multiplication

Let's now take a look at multiplying 1-digit numbers with 2-digit numbers.

Example:

$$17$$
$$\times \quad 3$$

The first step we take is to multiply the denominator (the bottom number) with the number directly above it (7).

Using our example we first multiply 3 x 7 and we get 21.

Next we take the 2-digit number and put the first number (2) on top of the number 1 from the numerator 17, so it looks like this:

$$\begin{array}{r} \overset{2}{1}7 \\ \times 3 \\ \hline 1 \end{array}$$

The final step is to now take the number 3 and multiply it with the first number in the numerator (1) and then add the number above it.

3 x 1 + 2 = 5

Therefore we put the 5 beside the number 1 under the question to the left, and now we have our answer! 51!

$$\begin{array}{r} \overset{2}{1}7 \\ \times 3 \\ \hline 51 \end{array}$$

Multiplication (1-digit x 2-digit)

Name: _____ Date: _____

2 x 10 =	3 x 14 =	4 x 18 =
2 x 11 =	3 x 15 =	4 x 19 =
2 x 12 =	3 x 16 =	5 x 10 =
2 x 13 =	3 x 17 =	5 x 11 =
2 x 14 =	3 x 18 =	5 x 12 =
2 x 15 =	3 x 19 =	5 x 13 =
2 x 16 =	4 x 10 =	5 x 14 =
2 x 17 =	4 x 11 =	5 x 15 =
2 x 18 =	4 x 12 =	5 x 16 =
2 x 19 =	4 x 13 =	5 x 17 =
3 x 10 =	4 x 14 =	5 x 18 =
3 x 11 =	4 x 15 =	5 x 19 =
3 x 12 =	4 x 16 =	
3 x 13 =	4 x 17 =	

Room for Solving

Multiplication (1-digit x 2-digit)

Name: _____ Date: _____

19 × 9	10 × 6	65 × 9	57 × 9
81 × 1	53 × 9	70 × 7	53 × 9
86 × 6	90 × 8	16 × 3	62 × 7
43 × 8	45 × 7	71 × 1	67 × 2
97 × 3	76 × 9	82 × 3	16 × 8

Room for Solving

Multiplication (1-digit x 2-digit)

Name: _____ Date: _____

71 × 2	66 × 7	17 × 1	17 × 6
58 × 2	62 × 4	45 × 8	53 × 7
39 × 7	52 × 7	25 × 3	41 × 7
71 × 2	22 × 1	59 × 7	79 × 4
21 × 8	61 × 8	11 × 9	87 × 5

Room for Solving

Multiplication (1-digit x 2-digit)

Name: _____ Date: _____

45 × 8	27 × 1	93 × 2	64 × 7
93 × 4	54 × 8	98 × 1	24 × 6
37 × 1	29 × 9	98 × 4	47 × 9
61 × 6	91 × 1	11 × 3	23 × 9
43 × 6	99 × 7	88 × 2	85 × 3

Room for
Solving

Multiplication (1-digit x 2-digit)

Name: _____ Date: _____

38 × 1	52 × 5	82 × 7	67 × 2
97 × 9	17 × 8	14 × 1	52 × 3
65 × 1	14 × 6	55 × 7	38 × 7
80 × 6	30 × 4	28 × 7	96 × 5
85 × 9	79 × 3	40 × 7	57 × 7

Room for Solving

Multiplication (1-digit x 2-digit)

Name: _____ Date: _____

25 × 9	95 × 8	24 × 4	79 × 6
19 × 4	26 × 5	48 × 7	33 × 6
47 × 9	88 × 8	26 × 2	50 × 8
75 × 8	41 × 7	70 × 1	87 × 7
25 × 6	44 × 8	57 × 6	53 × 3

Room for Solving

Multiplication (1-digit x 2-digit)

Name: _____ Date: _____

80 × 2	60 × 8	74 × 2	69 × 2
78 × 2	67 × 3	31 × 2	99 × 5
21 × 8	10 × 6	27 × 6	66 × 7
58 × 6	91 × 8	93 × 7	43 × 4
62 × 5	43 × 5	23 × 3	63 × 9

Room for Solving

3-digit x 2-digit Multiplication

Let's learn how to do grade 5 multiplication with 3 digits times 2 digits.

Example:

$$
\begin{array}{r}
637 \\
\times\ \ 48 \\
\hline
\end{array}
$$

Step 1: We first multiply the 8 with the 7 to get 56. We write down 6 in our first column and put the 5 on top of the next column so it looks like this:

$$
\begin{array}{r}
\overset{5}{6}37 \\
\times\ \ 48 \\
\hline
6
\end{array}
$$

Step 2: We now multiply the 8 with the next number, 3, and then add the number above it, 5. This equals 29. We write 9 beside 6 and put the 2 on top of the 6 in the numerator.

Now our equation looks like this:

$$\begin{array}{r} {}^{2}\ {}^{5}\ \\ 637 \\ \times\ \ 48 \\ \hline 96 \end{array}$$

Step 3: Now we multiply 8 with the last number, 6. We then take that number and add 2 to it. 8 x 6 + 2 = 50. We write 50 to finish off this row:

$$\begin{array}{r} {}^{2}\ {}^{5}\ \\ 637 \\ \times\ \ 48 \\ \hline 5096 \end{array}$$

Step 4: Now we go to the next number, 4. Since this number is in the "Tens" column, we must drop 1 zero under the number 6. Next, let's erase all the numbers above our numerator since we have already used all of them for our fist answer row. Your step should now look like this:

$$
\begin{array}{r}
6\overset{\,}{3}7 \\
\times\ \ 48 \\
\hline
5096 \\
0
\end{array}
$$

Step 5: Now we multiply the 4 with 7 to get 28, we place the 8 next to our bottom row answer, and place the 2 on top of the 3 in the numerator:

$$
\begin{array}{r}
6\overset{2}{3}7 \\
\times\ \ 48 \\
\hline
5096 \\
80
\end{array}
$$

Step 6: Now multiply the 4 with the 3 then add the 2 above it to get 14. We put the 1 on top of the 6 in the numerator and put the 4 beside our 8 in the 2ⁿᵈ answer row.

Step 7: Now we multiply the 4 with the 6 and add the 1 on top to get 25. We put the 25 beside the 4 in our 2nd answer row:

$$
\begin{array}{r}
{\scriptstyle 1\ 2} \\
6\overset{\cdot}{3}7 \\
\times\ \ 48 \\
\hline
5096 \\
25480 \\
\end{array}
$$

Step 8: Finally all we do now is add together both answer rows to get our final answer: 30,576

$$
\begin{array}{r}
{\scriptstyle 1\ 2} \\
6\overset{\cdot}{3}7 \\
\times\ \ 48 \\
\hline
5096 \\
+25480 \\
\hline
30576 \\
\end{array}
$$

Multiplication (3-digit x 2-digit)

Name: _____ Date: _____

20 x 101 =	30 x 145 =	40 x 189 =
20 x 112 =	30 x 156 =	40 x 190 =
20 x 123 =	30 x 167 =	50 x 101 =
20 x 134 =	30 x 178 =	50 x 112 =
20 x 145 =	30 x 189 =	50 x 123 =
20 x 156 =	30 x 190 =	50 x 134 =
20 x 167 =	40 x 101 =	50 x 145 =
20 x 178 =	40 x 112 =	50 x 156 =
20 x 189 =	40 x 123 =	50 x 167 =
20 x 190 =	40 x 134 =	50 x 178 =
30 x 101 =	40 x 145 =	50 x 189 =
30 x 112 =	40 x 156 =	50 x 190 =
30 x 123 =	40 x 167 =	
30 x 134 =	40 x 178 =	

Room for Solving

Multiplication (3-digit x 2-digit)

Name: _____ Date: _____

$$611 \times 81$$

$$986 \times 68$$

$$228 \times 72$$

$$257 \times 63$$

$$258 \times 95$$

$$268 \times 68$$

$$100 \times 16$$

$$432 \times 72$$

$$428 \times 75$$

$$772 \times 41$$

$$400 \times 23$$

$$397 \times 79$$

$$521 \times 48$$

$$766 \times 89$$

$$596 \times 90$$

$$308 \times 28$$

Room for Solving

Multiplication (3-digit x 2-digit)

Name: _____ Date: _____

$$413 \times 77$$

$$815 \times 66$$

$$205 \times 70$$

$$414 \times 65$$

$$348 \times 47$$

$$487 \times 86$$

$$740 \times 22$$

$$140 \times 64$$

$$221 \times 57$$

$$529 \times 68$$

$$812 \times 46$$

$$864 \times 75$$

$$844 \times 83$$

$$691 \times 27$$

$$532 \times 85$$

$$514 \times 75$$

Room for Solving

Multiplication (3-digit x 2-digit)

Name: _____ Date: _____

142	966	653	850
× 14	× 61	× 86	× 13

994	191	210	832
× 26	× 56	× 92	× 81

394	781	786	277
× 82	× 79	× 72	× 23

432	937	683	516
× 24	× 99	× 97	× 30

Room for Solving

Multiplication (3-digit x 2-digit)

Name: _____ Date: _____

396 × 38	843 × 83	427 × 55	486 × 57
122 × 41	543 × 57	509 × 90	155 × 67
969 × 14	394 × 96	290 × 45	517 × 63
870 × 28	321 × 21	320 × 69	148 × 65

Room for Solving

Multiplication (3-digit x 2-digit)

Name: _____ Date: _____

169 × 56	960 × 82	930 × 98	518 × 95
945 × 18	196 × 28	715 × 43	549 × 69
290 × 97	452 × 94	321 × 91	272 × 19
965 × 34	579 × 40	238 × 53	606 × 79

Room for Solving

Multiplication (3-digit x 2-digit)

Name: _____ Date: _____

116 × 86	300 × 49	210 × 63	143 × 98
598 × 46	646 × 71	606 × 93	340 × 63
376 × 51	417 × 15	990 × 43	393 × 81
985 × 88	955 × 54	678 × 78	227 × 28

Room for Solving

3rd, 4th and 5th Grade Division

Let's take a look at how to solve 2-digit & 1-digit numbers by 1-digit numbers:

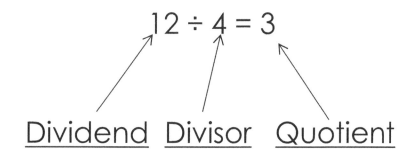

$$12 \div 4 = 3$$

<u>Dividend</u> <u>Divisor</u> <u>Quotient</u>

How do we divide $9 \div 3$?

1 way to look at it is to ask yourself which number time 3 equals 9?

$$3 \times ? = 9$$

This will give you the same answer as 9 ÷ 3

A second way to look at it is to group up the factors in the question:

Since the number we are dividing by is 9, let's say we have 9 circles:

Now all we have to figure out is how many groups of ● make 3?

There are 3 groups of 3, therefore 3 is our answer.

Division (1-digit & 2-digit ÷ 1-digit)

Name: _____ Date: _____

$7\overline{)49}$ $3\overline{)27}$ $3\overline{)18}$ $3\overline{)9}$

$9\overline{)63}$ $4\overline{)16}$ $2\overline{)6}$ $6\overline{)24}$

$7\overline{)42}$ $4\overline{)24}$ $8\overline{)24}$ $5\overline{)20}$

$7\overline{)14}$ $6\overline{)12}$ $7\overline{)21}$ $8\overline{)64}$

Room for Solving

Division (1-digit & 2-digit ÷ 1-digit)

$3\overline{)24}$ $2\overline{)18}$ $5\overline{)40}$ $7\overline{)42}$

$6\overline{)18}$ $3\overline{)21}$ $9\overline{)63}$ $6\overline{)54}$

$2\overline{)14}$ $2\overline{)16}$ $4\overline{)36}$ $5\overline{)10}$

$3\overline{)9}$ $2\overline{)10}$ $8\overline{)72}$ $4\overline{)20}$

Room for Solving

Division (1-digit & 2-digit ÷ 1-digit)

Name: _____ Date: _____

$9\overline{)45}$ $5\overline{)15}$ $9\overline{)27}$ $2\overline{)6}$

$4\overline{)8}$ $2\overline{)14}$ $6\overline{)30}$ $9\overline{)18}$

$5\overline{)25}$ $7\overline{)14}$ $3\overline{)21}$ $4\overline{)32}$

$7\overline{)28}$ $2\overline{)18}$ $8\overline{)48}$ $7\overline{)42}$

Room for Solving

Division (1-digit & 2-digit ÷ 1-digit)

Name: _____ Date: _____

$2 \overline{)14}$ $9 \overline{)36}$ $9 \overline{)81}$ $7 \overline{)56}$

$8 \overline{)64}$ $6 \overline{)36}$ $6 \overline{)18}$ $2 \overline{)8}$

$3 \overline{)21}$ $9 \overline{)18}$ $7 \overline{)42}$ $5 \overline{)35}$

$2 \overline{)18}$ $3 \overline{)24}$ $5 \overline{)10}$ $4 \overline{)28}$

Room for Solving

Division (1-digit & 2-digit ÷ 1-digit)

Name: _____ Date: _____

$4 \overline{)8}$ $9 \overline{)36}$ $5 \overline{)10}$ $2 \overline{)6}$

$7 \overline{)42}$ $5 \overline{)25}$ $3 \overline{)15}$ $7 \overline{)49}$

$3 \overline{)12}$ $9 \overline{)27}$ $3 \overline{)6}$ $2 \overline{)12}$

$7 \overline{)63}$ $2 \overline{)8}$ $3 \overline{)18}$ $4 \overline{)16}$

Room for Solving

Division (1-digit & 2-digit ÷ 1-digit)

Name: _____ Date: _____

2)10   5)30   4)24   6)12

8)24   9)63   2)8   4)12

7)21   2)14   7)56   4)16

4)32   9)54   5)40   8)40

Room for Solving

Division (1-digit & 2-digit ÷ 1-digit)

Name: _____ Date: _____

$$5\overline{)15} \qquad 3\overline{)21} \qquad 8\overline{)24} \qquad 8\overline{)32}$$

$$2\overline{)12} \qquad 6\overline{)30} \qquad 4\overline{)28} \qquad 2\overline{)8}$$

$$5\overline{)45} \qquad 6\overline{)24} \qquad 5\overline{)30} \qquad 6\overline{)18}$$

$$2\overline{)16} \qquad 4\overline{)36} \qquad 9\overline{)36} \qquad 8\overline{)40}$$

Room for Solving

Division (1-digit & 2-digit ÷ 1-digit)

Name: _____ Date: _____

$45 \div 5 =$	$30 \div 5 =$	$4 \div 4 =$	$7 \div 1 =$	$10 \div 5 =$
$27 \div 3 =$	$6 \div 2 =$	$48 \div 6 =$	$12 \div 6 =$	$0 \div 5 =$
$72 \div 8 =$	$16 \div 4 =$	$6 \div 6 =$	$9 \div 9 =$	$12 \div 2 =$
$0 \div 4 =$	$36 \div 9 =$	$5 \div 5 =$	$32 \div 4 =$	$14 \div 7 =$
$3 \div 3 =$	$8 \div 8 =$	$45 \div 9 =$	$48 \div 8 =$	$36 \div 6 =$
$20 \div 5 =$	$25 \div 5 =$	$9 \div 3 =$	$6 \div 3 =$	$5 \div 1 =$
$0 \div 3 =$	$15 \div 5 =$	$32 \div 8 =$	$18 \div 9 =$	$2 \div 1 =$
$8 \div 2 =$	$40 \div 8 =$	$9 \div 1 =$	$81 \div 9 =$	$0 \div 8 =$
$63 \div 7 =$	$16 \div 2 =$	$35 \div 5 =$	$4 \div 1 =$	$0 \div 7 =$
$27 \div 9 =$	$54 \div 6 =$	$0 \div 6 =$	$8 \div 1 =$	$30 \div 6 =$
$15 \div 3 =$	$3 \div 1 =$	$18 \div 6 =$	$1 \div 1 =$	$21 \div 3 =$
$0 \div 1 =$	$4 \div 2 =$	$10 \div 2 =$	$21 \div 7 =$	$35 \div 7 =$
$24 \div 4 =$	$54 \div 9 =$	$64 \div 8 =$	$24 \div 6 =$	$42 \div 7 =$
$42 \div 6 =$	$28 \div 4 =$	$49 \div 7 =$	$36 \div 4 =$	$12 \div 4 =$
$72 \div 9 =$	$18 \div 2 =$	$18 \div 3 =$	$2 \div 2 =$	$56 \div 7 =$
$24 \div 3 =$	$14 \div 2 =$	$0 \div 2 =$	$16 \div 8 =$	$24 \div 8 =$

Room for Solving

Division (3-digit ÷ 2-digit)

Name: _____ Date: _____

$22\overline{)134}$ $24\overline{)166}$ $21\overline{)193}$

$34\overline{)170}$ $46\overline{)260}$ $86\overline{)702}$

$65\overline{)520}$ $68\overline{)551}$ $35\overline{)175}$

$76\overline{)485}$ $79\overline{)699}$ $93\overline{)847}$

Room for Solving

Division (3-digit ÷ 2-digit)

$78\overline{)546}$ $16\overline{)77}$ $34\overline{)217}$

$47\overline{)164}$ $92\overline{)237}$ $35\overline{)280}$

$96\overline{)288}$ $61\overline{)427}$ $81\overline{)560}$

$93\overline{)361}$ $59\overline{)402}$ $38\overline{)342}$

Room for Solving

Division (3-digit ÷ 2-digit)

Name: _____ Date: _____

$73\overline{)219}$ $16\overline{)59}$ $93\overline{)186}$

$66\overline{)264}$ $99\overline{)297}$ $53\overline{)477}$

$32\overline{)128}$ $49\overline{)441}$ $14\overline{)99}$

$21\overline{)42}$ $47\overline{)282}$ $28\overline{)168}$

Room for Solving

Division (3-digit ÷ 2-digit)

Name: _____ Date: _____

$$43\overline{)344} \qquad 78\overline{)468} \qquad 96\overline{)435}$$

$$63\overline{)252} \qquad 63\overline{)315} \qquad 78\overline{)572}$$

$$92\overline{)644} \qquad 51\overline{)113} \qquad 92\overline{)644}$$

$$28\overline{)140} \qquad 41\overline{)220} \qquad 73\overline{)438}$$

Room for Solving

Division (3-digit ÷ 2-digit)

Name: _____ Date: _____

$83\overline{)410}$ $\qquad$ $13\overline{)84}$ $\qquad$ $35\overline{)334}$

$84\overline{)171}$ $\qquad$ $82\overline{)492}$ $\qquad$ $19\overline{)133}$

$26\overline{)192}$ $\qquad$ $16\overline{)130}$ $\qquad$ $33\overline{)108}$

$91\overline{)289}$ $\qquad$ $18\overline{)128}$ $\qquad$ $55\overline{)220}$

Room for Solving

Answer Key

Pg. 7 & 8

Basic Multiplication (2x to 5x)

2 x 1 = **2**	3 x 4 = **12**	4 x 7 = **28**
2 x 2 = **4**	3 x 5 = **15**	4 x 8 = **32**
2 x 3 = **6**	3 x 6 = **18**	4 x 9 = **36**
2 x 4 = **8**	3 x 7 = **21**	5 x 1 = **5**
2 x 5 = **10**	3 x 8 = **24**	5 x 2 = **10**
2 x 6 = **12**	3 x 9 = **27**	5 x 3 = **15**
2 x 7 = **14**	4 x 1 = **4**	5 x 4 = **20**
2 x 8 = **16**	4 x 2 = **8**	5 x 5 = **25**
2 x 9= **18**	4 x 3 = **12**	5 x 6 = **30**
3 x 1 = **3**	4 x 4 = **16**	5 x 7 = **35**
3 x 2 = **6**	4 x 5 = **20**	5 x 8 = **40**
3 x 3 = **9**	4 x 6 = **24**	5 x 9 = **45**

Basic Multiplication (6x to 9x)

6 x 1 = **6**	7 x 4 = **28**	8 x 7 = **56**
6 x 2 = **12**	7 x 5 = **35**	8 x 8 = **64**
6 x 3 = **18**	7 x 6 = **42**	8 x 9 = **72**
6 x 4 = **24**	7 x 7 = **49**	9 x 1 = **9**
6 x 5 = **30**	7 x 8 = **56**	9 x 2 = **18**
6 x 6 = **36**	7 x 9 = **63**	9 x 3 = **27**
6 x 7 = **42**	8 x 1 = **8**	9 x 4 = **36**
6 x 8 = **48**	8 x 2 = **16**	9 x 5 = **45**
6 x 9 = **54**	8 x 3 = **24**	9 x 6 = **54**
7 x 1 = **7**	8 x 4 = **32**	9 x 7 = **63**
7 x 2 = **14**	8 x 5 = **40**	9 x 8 = **72**
7 x 3 = **21**	8 x 6 = **48**	9 x 9 = **81**

8 × 6 **48**	8 × 9 **72**	2 × 8 **16**	4 × 6 **24**	3 × 8 **24**
3 × 4 **12**	5 × 2 **10**	6 × 3 **18**	6 × 4 **24**	8 × 8 **64**
5 × 6 **30**	8 × 5 **40**	5 × 1 **5**	4 × 2 **8**	7 × 9 **63**
3 × 6 **18**	9 × 2 **18**	3 × 5 **15**	2 × 2 **4**	6 × 2 **12**
5 × 7 **35**	3 × 7 **21**	4 × 4 **16**	8 × 7 **56**	3 × 3 **9**

2 × 3 **6**	7 × 1 **7**	8 × 8 **64**	6 × 8 **48**	2 × 8 **16**
2 × 2 **4**	6 × 1 **6**	2 × 5 **10**	6 × 4 **24**	3 × 1 **3**
4 × 9 **36**	2 × 6 **12**	6 × 5 **30**	1 × 8 **8**	9 × 4 **36**
4 × 4 **16**	8 × 7 **56**	5 × 8 **40**	1 × 6 **6**	2 × 4 **8**
4 × 7 **28**	1 × 3 **3**	3 × 4 **12**	6 × 6 **36**	9 × 5 **45**

Pg. 13

10	10	7	3	2
x 2	x 4	x 10	x 10	x 1
20	40	70	30	2

3	1	8	4	1
x 9	x 8	x 6	x 8	x 2
27	8	48	32	2

3	10	9	9	8
x 7	x 8	x 2	x 10	x 10
21	80	18	90	80

6	4	4	10	3
x 10	x 3	x 6	x 6	x 5
60	12	24	60	15

1	9	1	1	2
x 7	x 1	x 5	x 10	x 5
7	9	5	10	10

Pg. 15

9	7	9	3	2
x 2	x 2	x 4	x 3	x 7
18	14	36	9	14

5	10	4	7	5
x 10	x 8	x 2	x 4	x 9
50	80	8	28	45

6	6	7	8	8
x 5	x 2	x 7	x 3	x 7
30	12	49	24	56

10	5	9	2	3
x 3	x 5	x 10	x 5	x 7
30	25	90	10	21

10	4	2	5	6
x 6	x 6	x 3	x 4	x 4
60	24	6	20	24

Pg. 17

9 × 7 **63**	10 × 6 **60**	4 × 2 **8**	7 × 4 **28**	10 × 5 **50**
3 × 2 **6**	4 × 8 **32**	7 × 7 **49**	7 × 2 **14**	9 × 4 **36**
3 × 4 **12**	5 × 7 **35**	4 × 5 **20**	8 × 3 **24**	10 × 8 **80**
4 × 4 **16**	9 × 3 **27**	8 × 6 **48**	8 × 7 **56**	5 × 3 **15**
6 × 4 **24**	5 × 5 **25**	5 × 10 **50**	3 × 5 **15**	10 × 3 **30**

Pg. 19

5 × 6 **30**	5 × 8 **40**	10 × 1 **10**	9 × 1 **9**	2 × 1 **2**
1 × 9 **9**	7 × 4 **28**	6 × 8 **48**	9 × 2 **18**	5 × 10 **50**
7 × 7 **49**	5 × 7 **35**	8 × 5 **40**	1 × 8 **8**	10 × 10 **100**
3 × 6 **18**	1 × 2 **2**	3 × 3 **9**	3 × 10 **30**	4 × 8 **32**
5 × 0 **0**	5 × 9 **45**	6 × 10 **60**	4 × 4 **16**	9 × 8 **72**

Pg. 23

Multiplication (1-digit x 2-digit)

Name: _____ Date: _____

2 x 10 = 20	3 x 14 = 42	4 x 18 = 72
2 x 11 = 22	3 x 15 = 45	4 x 19 = 76
2 x 12 = 24	3 x 16 = 48	5 x 10 = 50
2 x 13 = 26	3 x 17 = 51	5 x 11 = 55
2 x 14 = 28	3 x 18 = 54	5 x 12 = 60
2 x 15 = 30	3 x 19 = 57	5 x 13 = 65
2 x 16 = 32	4 x 10 = 40	5 x 14 = 70
2 x 17 = 34	4 x 11 = 44	5 x 15 = 75
2 x 18 = 36	4 x 12 = 48	5 x 16 = 80
2 x 19 = 38	4 x 13 = 52	5 x 17 = 85
3 x 10 = 30	4 x 14 = 56	5 x 18 = 90
3 x 11 = 33	4 x 15 = 60	5 x 19 = 95
3 x 12 = 36	4 x 16 = 64	
3 x 13 = 39	4 x 17 = 68	

Pg. 25

```
  19        10        65        57
×  9      ×  6      ×  9      ×  9
─────     ─────     ─────     ─────
 171        60       585       513


  81        53        70        53
×  1      ×  9      ×  7      ×  9
─────     ─────     ─────     ─────
  81       477       490       477


  86        90        16        62
×  6      ×  8      ×  3      ×  7
─────     ─────     ─────     ─────
 516       720        48       434


  43        45        71        67
×  8      ×  7      ×  1      ×  2
─────     ─────     ─────     ─────
 344       315        71       134


  97        76        82        16
×  3      ×  9      ×  3      ×  8
─────     ─────     ─────     ─────
 291       684       246       128
```

Pg. 27

71 × 2 142	66 × 7 462	17 × 1 17	17 × 6 102
58 × 2 116	62 × 4 248	45 × 8 360	53 × 7 371
39 × 7 273	52 × 7 364	25 × 3 75	41 × 7 287
71 × 2 142	22 × 1 22	59 × 7 413	79 × 4 316
21 × 8 168	61 × 8 488	11 × 9 99	87 × 5 435

Pg. 29

45 × 8 360	27 × 1 27	93 × 2 186	64 × 7 448
93 × 4 372	54 × 8 432	98 × 1 98	24 × 6 144
37 × 1 37	29 × 9 261	98 × 4 392	47 × 9 423
61 × 6 366	91 × 1 91	11 × 3 33	23 × 9 207
43 × 6 258	99 × 7 693	88 × 2 176	85 × 3 255

Pg. 31

38 × 1 38	52 × 5 260	82 × 7 574	67 × 2 134
97 × 9 873	17 × 8 136	14 × 1 14	52 × 3 156
65 × 1 65	14 × 6 84	55 × 7 385	38 × 7 266
80 × 6 480	30 × 4 120	28 × 7 196	96 × 5 480
85 × 9 765	79 × 3 237	40 × 7 280	57 × 7 399

Pg. 33

25 × 9 225	95 × 8 760	24 × 4 96	79 × 6 474
19 × 4 76	26 × 5 130	48 × 7 336	33 × 6 198
47 × 9 423	88 × 8 704	26 × 2 52	50 × 8 400
75 × 8 600	41 × 7 287	70 × 1 70	87 × 7 609
25 × 6 150	44 × 8 352	57 × 6 342	53 × 3 159

Pg. 35

80 × 2 160	60 × 8 480	74 × 2 148	69 × 2 138
78 × 2 156	67 × 3 201	31 × 2 62	99 × 5 495
21 × 8 168	10 × 6 60	27 × 6 162	66 × 7 462
58 × 6 348	91 × 8 728	93 × 7 651	43 × 4 172
62 × 5 310	43 × 5 215	23 × 3 69	63 × 9 567

Pg. 41

Multiplication (3-digit x 2-digit)

Name: _____ Date: _____

20 x 101 = **2020**	30 x 145 = **4350**	40 x 189 = **7560**
20 x 112 = **2240**	30 x 156 = **4680**	40 x 190 = **7600**
20 x 123 = **2460**	30 x 167 = **5010**	50 x 101 = **5050**
20 x 134 = **2680**	30 x 178 = **5340**	50 x 112 = **5600**
20 x 145 = **2900**	30 x 189 = **5670**	50 x 123 = **6150**
20 x 156 = **3120**	30 x 190 = **5700**	50 x 134 = **6700**
20 x 167 = **3340**	40 x 101 = **4040**	50 x 145 = **7250**
20 x 178 = **3560**	40 x 112 = **4480**	50 x 156 = **7800**
20 x 189 = **3780**	40 x 123 = **4920**	50 x 167 = **8350**
20 x 190 = **3800**	40 x 134 = **5360**	50 x 178 = **8900**
30 x 101 = **3030**	40 x 145 = **5800**	50 x 189 = **9450**
30 x 112 = **3360**	40 x 156 = **6240**	50 x 190 = **9500**
30 x 123 = **3690**	40 x 167 = **6680**	
30 x 134 = **4020**	40 x 178 = **7120**	

Pg. 43

611	986	228	257
× 81	× 68	× 72	× 63
611	7888	456	771
48880	59160	15960	15420
49491	67048	16416	16191

258	268	100	432
× 95	× 68	× 16	× 72
1290	2144	600	864
23220	16080	1000	30240
24510	18224	1600	31104

428	772	400	397
× 75	× 41	× 23	× 79
2140	772	1200	3573
29960	30880	8000	27790
32100	31652	9200	31363

521	766	596	308
× 48	× 89	× 90	× 28
4168	6894	53640	2464
20840	61280		6160
25008	68174		8624

Pg. 45

413	815	205	414
× 77	× 66	× 70	× 65
2891	4890	14350	2070
28910	48900		24840
31801	53790		26910

348	487	740	140
× 47	× 86	× 22	× 64
2436	2922	1480	560
13920	38960	14800	8400
16356	41882	16280	8960

221	529	812	864
× 57	× 68	× 46	× 75
1547	4232	4872	4320
11050	31740	32480	60480
12597	35972	37352	64800

844	691	532	514
× 83	× 27	× 85	× 75
2532	4837	2660	2570
67520	13820	42560	35980
70052	18657	45220	38550

Pg. 47

142	966	653	850
× 14	× 61	× 86	× 13
568	966	3918	2550
1420	57960	52240	8500
1988	58926	56158	11050

994	191	210	832
× 26	× 56	× 92	× 81
5964	1146	420	832
19880	9550	18900	66560
25844	10696	19320	67392

394	781	786	277
× 82	× 79	× 72	× 23
788	7029	1572	831
31520	54670	55020	5540
32308	61699	56592	6371

432	937	683	516
× 24	× 99	× 97	× 30
1728	8433	4781	15480
8640	84330	61470	
10368	92763	66251	

Pg. 49

396	843	427	486
× 38	× 83	× 55	× 57
3168	2529	2135	3402
11880	67440	21350	24300
15048	69969	23485	27702

122	543	509	155
× 41	× 57	× 90	× 67
122	3801	45810	1085
4880	27150		9300
5002	30951		10385

969	394	290	517
× 14	× 96	× 45	× 63
3876	2364	1450	1551
9690	35460	11600	31020
13566	37824	13050	32571

870	321	320	148
× 28	× 21	× 69	× 65
6960	321	2880	740
17400	6420	19200	8880
24360	6741	22080	9620

Pg. 51

```
  169      960      930      518
×  56    ×  82    ×  98    ×  95
 1014     1920     7440     2590
 8450    76800    83700    46620
 9464    78720    91140    49210


  945      196      715      549
×  18    ×  28    ×  43    ×  69
 7560     1568     2145     4941
 9450     3920    28600    32940
17010     5488    30745    37881


  290      452      321      272
×  97    ×  94    ×  91    ×  19
 2030     1808      321     2448
26100    40680    28890     2720
28130    42488    29211     5168


  965      579      238      606
×  34    ×  40    ×  53    ×  79
 3860    23160      714     5454
28950            11900    42420
32810            12614    47874
```

Pg. 53

```
  116      300      210      143
×  86    ×  49    ×  63    ×  98
  696     2700      630     1144
 9280    12000    12600    12870
 9976    14700    13230    14014


  598      646      606      340
×  46    ×  71    ×  93    ×  63
 3588      646     1818     1020
23920    45220    54540    20400
27508    45866    56358    21420


  376      417      990      393
×  51    ×  15    ×  43    ×  81
  376     2085     2970      393
18800     4170    39600    31440
19176     6255    42570    31833


  985      955      678      227
×  88    ×  54    ×  78    ×  28
 7880     3820     5424     1816
78800    47750    47460     4540
86680    51570    52884     6356
```

Pg. 57

$$\begin{array}{r} 7 \\ 7\overline{)49} \\ \underline{49} \\ 0 \end{array}$$
$$\begin{array}{r} 9 \\ 3\overline{)27} \\ \underline{27} \\ 0 \end{array}$$
$$\begin{array}{r} 6 \\ 3\overline{)18} \\ \underline{18} \\ 0 \end{array}$$
$$\begin{array}{r} 3 \\ 3\overline{)9} \\ \underline{9} \\ 0 \end{array}$$

$$\begin{array}{r} 7 \\ 9\overline{)63} \\ \underline{63} \\ 0 \end{array}$$
$$\begin{array}{r} 4 \\ 4\overline{)16} \\ \underline{16} \\ 0 \end{array}$$
$$\begin{array}{r} 3 \\ 2\overline{)6} \\ \underline{6} \\ 0 \end{array}$$
$$\begin{array}{r} 4 \\ 6\overline{)24} \\ \underline{24} \\ 0 \end{array}$$

$$\begin{array}{r} 6 \\ 7\overline{)42} \\ \underline{42} \\ 0 \end{array}$$
$$\begin{array}{r} 6 \\ 4\overline{)24} \\ \underline{24} \\ 0 \end{array}$$
$$\begin{array}{r} 3 \\ 8\overline{)24} \\ \underline{24} \\ 0 \end{array}$$
$$\begin{array}{r} 4 \\ 5\overline{)20} \\ \underline{20} \\ 0 \end{array}$$

$$\begin{array}{r} 2 \\ 7\overline{)14} \\ \underline{14} \\ 0 \end{array}$$
$$\begin{array}{r} 2 \\ 6\overline{)12} \\ \underline{12} \\ 0 \end{array}$$
$$\begin{array}{r} 3 \\ 7\overline{)21} \\ \underline{21} \\ 0 \end{array}$$
$$\begin{array}{r} 8 \\ 8\overline{)64} \\ \underline{64} \\ 0 \end{array}$$

Pg. 59

$$\begin{array}{r} 8 \\ 3\overline{)24} \\ \underline{24} \\ 0 \end{array}$$
$$\begin{array}{r} 9 \\ 2\overline{)18} \\ \underline{18} \\ 0 \end{array}$$
$$\begin{array}{r} 8 \\ 5\overline{)40} \\ \underline{40} \\ 0 \end{array}$$
$$\begin{array}{r} 6 \\ 7\overline{)42} \\ \underline{42} \\ 0 \end{array}$$

$$\begin{array}{r} 3 \\ 6\overline{)18} \\ \underline{18} \\ 0 \end{array}$$
$$\begin{array}{r} 7 \\ 3\overline{)21} \\ \underline{21} \\ 0 \end{array}$$
$$\begin{array}{r} 7 \\ 9\overline{)63} \\ \underline{63} \\ 0 \end{array}$$
$$\begin{array}{r} 9 \\ 6\overline{)54} \\ \underline{54} \\ 0 \end{array}$$

$$\begin{array}{r} 7 \\ 2\overline{)14} \\ \underline{14} \\ 0 \end{array}$$
$$\begin{array}{r} 8 \\ 2\overline{)16} \\ \underline{16} \\ 0 \end{array}$$
$$\begin{array}{r} 9 \\ 4\overline{)36} \\ \underline{36} \\ 0 \end{array}$$
$$\begin{array}{r} 2 \\ 5\overline{)10} \\ \underline{10} \\ 0 \end{array}$$

$$\begin{array}{r} 3 \\ 3\overline{)9} \\ \underline{9} \\ 0 \end{array}$$
$$\begin{array}{r} 5 \\ 2\overline{)10} \\ \underline{10} \\ 0 \end{array}$$
$$\begin{array}{r} 9 \\ 8\overline{)72} \\ \underline{72} \\ 0 \end{array}$$
$$\begin{array}{r} 5 \\ 4\overline{)20} \\ \underline{20} \\ 0 \end{array}$$

Pg. 61

$$\begin{array}{r}5\\9\overline{)45}\\45\\\hline 0\end{array}\qquad\begin{array}{r}3\\5\overline{)15}\\15\\\hline 0\end{array}\qquad\begin{array}{r}3\\9\overline{)27}\\27\\\hline 0\end{array}\qquad\begin{array}{r}3\\2\overline{)6}\\6\\\hline 0\end{array}$$

$$\begin{array}{r}2\\4\overline{)8}\\8\\\hline 0\end{array}\qquad\begin{array}{r}7\\2\overline{)14}\\14\\\hline 0\end{array}\qquad\begin{array}{r}5\\6\overline{)30}\\30\\\hline 0\end{array}\qquad\begin{array}{r}2\\9\overline{)18}\\18\\\hline 0\end{array}$$

$$\begin{array}{r}5\\5\overline{)25}\\25\\\hline 0\end{array}\qquad\begin{array}{r}2\\7\overline{)14}\\14\\\hline 0\end{array}\qquad\begin{array}{r}7\\3\overline{)21}\\21\\\hline 0\end{array}\qquad\begin{array}{r}8\\4\overline{)32}\\32\\\hline 0\end{array}$$

$$\begin{array}{r}4\\7\overline{)28}\\28\\\hline 0\end{array}\qquad\begin{array}{r}9\\2\overline{)18}\\18\\\hline 0\end{array}\qquad\begin{array}{r}6\\8\overline{)48}\\48\\\hline 0\end{array}\qquad\begin{array}{r}6\\7\overline{)42}\\42\\\hline 0\end{array}$$

Pg. 63

$$\begin{array}{r}7\\2\overline{)14}\\14\\\hline 0\end{array}\qquad\begin{array}{r}4\\9\overline{)36}\\36\\\hline 0\end{array}\qquad\begin{array}{r}9\\9\overline{)81}\\81\\\hline 0\end{array}\qquad\begin{array}{r}8\\7\overline{)56}\\56\\\hline 0\end{array}$$

$$\begin{array}{r}8\\8\overline{)64}\\64\\\hline 0\end{array}\qquad\begin{array}{r}6\\6\overline{)36}\\36\\\hline 0\end{array}\qquad\begin{array}{r}3\\6\overline{)18}\\18\\\hline 0\end{array}\qquad\begin{array}{r}4\\2\overline{)8}\\8\\\hline 0\end{array}$$

$$\begin{array}{r}7\\3\overline{)21}\\21\\\hline 0\end{array}\qquad\begin{array}{r}2\\9\overline{)18}\\18\\\hline 0\end{array}\qquad\begin{array}{r}6\\7\overline{)42}\\42\\\hline 0\end{array}\qquad\begin{array}{r}7\\5\overline{)35}\\35\\\hline 0\end{array}$$

$$\begin{array}{r}9\\2\overline{)18}\\18\\\hline 0\end{array}\qquad\begin{array}{r}8\\3\overline{)24}\\24\\\hline 0\end{array}\qquad\begin{array}{r}2\\5\overline{)10}\\10\\\hline 0\end{array}\qquad\begin{array}{r}7\\4\overline{)28}\\28\\\hline 0\end{array}$$

Pg. 65

$$
\begin{array}{r} 2 \\ 4\overline{)8} \\ \underline{8} \\ 0 \end{array}
\qquad
\begin{array}{r} 4 \\ 9\overline{)36} \\ \underline{36} \\ 0 \end{array}
\qquad
\begin{array}{r} 2 \\ 5\overline{)10} \\ \underline{10} \\ 0 \end{array}
\qquad
\begin{array}{r} 3 \\ 2\overline{)6} \\ \underline{6} \\ 0 \end{array}
$$

$$
\begin{array}{r} 6 \\ 7\overline{)42} \\ \underline{42} \\ 0 \end{array}
\qquad
\begin{array}{r} 5 \\ 5\overline{)25} \\ \underline{25} \\ 0 \end{array}
\qquad
\begin{array}{r} 5 \\ 3\overline{)15} \\ \underline{15} \\ 0 \end{array}
\qquad
\begin{array}{r} 7 \\ 7\overline{)49} \\ \underline{49} \\ 0 \end{array}
$$

$$
\begin{array}{r} 4 \\ 3\overline{)12} \\ \underline{12} \\ 0 \end{array}
\qquad
\begin{array}{r} 3 \\ 9\overline{)27} \\ \underline{27} \\ 0 \end{array}
\qquad
\begin{array}{r} 2 \\ 3\overline{)6} \\ \underline{6} \\ 0 \end{array}
\qquad
\begin{array}{r} 6 \\ 2\overline{)12} \\ \underline{12} \\ 0 \end{array}
$$

$$
\begin{array}{r} 9 \\ 7\overline{)63} \\ \underline{63} \\ 0 \end{array}
\qquad
\begin{array}{r} 4 \\ 2\overline{)8} \\ \underline{8} \\ 0 \end{array}
\qquad
\begin{array}{r} 6 \\ 3\overline{)18} \\ \underline{18} \\ 0 \end{array}
\qquad
\begin{array}{r} 4 \\ 4\overline{)16} \\ \underline{16} \\ 0 \end{array}
$$

Pg. 67

$$
\begin{array}{r} 5 \\ 2\overline{)10} \\ \underline{10} \\ 0 \end{array}
\qquad
\begin{array}{r} 6 \\ 5\overline{)30} \\ \underline{30} \\ 0 \end{array}
\qquad
\begin{array}{r} 6 \\ 4\overline{)24} \\ \underline{24} \\ 0 \end{array}
\qquad
\begin{array}{r} 2 \\ 6\overline{)12} \\ \underline{12} \\ 0 \end{array}
$$

$$
\begin{array}{r} 3 \\ 8\overline{)24} \\ \underline{24} \\ 0 \end{array}
\qquad
\begin{array}{r} 7 \\ 9\overline{)63} \\ \underline{63} \\ 0 \end{array}
\qquad
\begin{array}{r} 4 \\ 2\overline{)8} \\ \underline{8} \\ 0 \end{array}
\qquad
\begin{array}{r} 3 \\ 4\overline{)12} \\ \underline{12} \\ 0 \end{array}
$$

$$
\begin{array}{r} 3 \\ 7\overline{)21} \\ \underline{21} \\ 0 \end{array}
\qquad
\begin{array}{r} 7 \\ 2\overline{)14} \\ \underline{14} \\ 0 \end{array}
\qquad
\begin{array}{r} 8 \\ 7\overline{)56} \\ \underline{56} \\ 0 \end{array}
\qquad
\begin{array}{r} 4 \\ 4\overline{)16} \\ \underline{16} \\ 0 \end{array}
$$

$$
\begin{array}{r} 8 \\ 4\overline{)32} \\ \underline{32} \\ 0 \end{array}
\qquad
\begin{array}{r} 6 \\ 9\overline{)54} \\ \underline{54} \\ 0 \end{array}
\qquad
\begin{array}{r} 8 \\ 5\overline{)40} \\ \underline{40} \\ 0 \end{array}
\qquad
\begin{array}{r} 5 \\ 8\overline{)40} \\ \underline{40} \\ 0 \end{array}
$$

$$\begin{array}{r} 3 \\ 5\overline{)15} \\ 15 \\ \hline 0 \end{array} \qquad \begin{array}{r} 7 \\ 3\overline{)21} \\ 21 \\ \hline 0 \end{array} \qquad \begin{array}{r} 3 \\ 8\overline{)24} \\ 24 \\ \hline 0 \end{array} \qquad \begin{array}{r} 4 \\ 8\overline{)32} \\ 32 \\ \hline 0 \end{array}$$

$$\begin{array}{r} 6 \\ 2\overline{)12} \\ 12 \\ \hline 0 \end{array} \qquad \begin{array}{r} 5 \\ 6\overline{)30} \\ 30 \\ \hline 0 \end{array} \qquad \begin{array}{r} 7 \\ 4\overline{)28} \\ 28 \\ \hline 0 \end{array} \qquad \begin{array}{r} 4 \\ 2\overline{)8} \\ 8 \\ \hline 0 \end{array}$$

$$\begin{array}{r} 9 \\ 5\overline{)45} \\ 45 \\ \hline 0 \end{array} \qquad \begin{array}{r} 4 \\ 6\overline{)24} \\ 24 \\ \hline 0 \end{array} \qquad \begin{array}{r} 6 \\ 5\overline{)30} \\ 30 \\ \hline 0 \end{array} \qquad \begin{array}{r} 3 \\ 6\overline{)18} \\ 18 \\ \hline 0 \end{array}$$

$$\begin{array}{r} 8 \\ 2\overline{)16} \\ 16 \\ \hline 0 \end{array} \qquad \begin{array}{r} 9 \\ 4\overline{)36} \\ 36 \\ \hline 0 \end{array} \qquad \begin{array}{r} 4 \\ 9\overline{)36} \\ 36 \\ \hline 0 \end{array} \qquad \begin{array}{r} 5 \\ 8\overline{)40} \\ 40 \\ \hline 0 \end{array}$$

Pg. 71

$45 \div 5 = 9$	$30 \div 5 = 6$	$4 \div 4 = 1$	$7 \div 1 = 7$	$10 \div 5 = 2$
$27 \div 3 = 9$	$6 \div 2 = 3$	$48 \div 6 = 8$	$12 \div 6 = 2$	$0 \div 5 = 0$
$72 \div 8 = 9$	$16 \div 4 = 4$	$6 \div 6 = 1$	$9 \div 9 = 1$	$12 \div 2 = 6$
$0 \div 4 = 0$	$36 \div 9 = 4$	$5 \div 5 = 1$	$32 \div 4 = 8$	$14 \div 7 = 2$
$3 \div 3 = 1$	$8 \div 8 = 1$	$45 \div 9 = 5$	$48 \div 8 = 6$	$36 \div 6 = 6$
$20 \div 5 = 4$	$25 \div 5 = 5$	$9 \div 3 = 3$	$6 \div 3 = 2$	$5 \div 1 = 5$
$0 \div 3 = 0$	$15 \div 5 = 3$	$32 \div 8 = 4$	$18 \div 9 = 2$	$2 \div 1 = 2$
$8 \div 2 = 4$	$40 \div 8 = 5$	$9 \div 1 = 9$	$81 \div 9 = 9$	$0 \div 8 = 0$
$63 \div 7 = 9$	$16 \div 2 = 8$	$35 \div 5 = 7$	$4 \div 1 = 4$	$0 \div 7 = 0$
$27 \div 9 = 3$	$54 \div 6 = 9$	$0 \div 6 = 0$	$8 \div 1 = 8$	$30 \div 6 = 5$
$15 \div 3 = 5$	$3 \div 1 = 3$	$18 \div 6 = 3$	$1 \div 1 = 1$	$21 \div 3 = 7$
$0 \div 1 = 0$	$4 \div 2 = 2$	$10 \div 2 = 5$	$21 \div 7 = 3$	$35 \div 7 = 5$
$24 \div 4 = 6$	$54 \div 9 = 6$	$64 \div 8 = 8$	$24 \div 6 = 4$	$42 \div 7 = 6$
$42 \div 6 = 7$	$28 \div 4 = 7$	$49 \div 7 = 7$	$36 \div 4 = 9$	$12 \div 4 = 3$
$72 \div 9 = 8$	$18 \div 2 = 9$	$18 \div 3 = 6$	$2 \div 2 = 1$	$56 \div 7 = 8$
$24 \div 3 = 8$	$14 \div 2 = 7$	$0 \div 2 = 0$	$16 \div 8 = 2$	$24 \div 8 = 3$

Pg. 73

```
        6 r 2              6 r 22             9 r 4
22 ) 134          24 ) 166           21 ) 193
     132               144                189
       2                22                  4


         5              5 r 30             8 r 14
34 ) 170          46 ) 260           86 ) 702
     170               230                688
       0                30                 14


         8              8 r 7                5
65 ) 520          68 ) 551           35 ) 175
     520               544                175
       0                 7                  0


        6 r 29           8 r 67             9 r 10
76 ) 485          79 ) 699           93 ) 847
     456               632                837
      29                67                 10
```

Pg. 75

```
         7              4 r 13             6 r 13
78 ) 546          16 ) 77            34 ) 217
     546               64                 204
       0                13                 13


        3 r 23           2 r 53              8
47 ) 164          92 ) 237           35 ) 280
     141               184                280
      23                53                  0


         3                7               6 r 74
96 ) 288          61 ) 427           81 ) 560
     288               427                486
       0                 0                 74


        3 r 82           6 r 48              9
93 ) 361          59 ) 402           38 ) 342
     279               354                342
      82                48                  0
```

Pg. 77

```
        3              3r 11           2
    73)219          16)59          93)186
      219             48             186
        0             11               0


        4              3              9
    66)264          99)297         53)477
      264            297            477
        0              0              0


        4              9            7r 1
    32)128          49)441         14)99
      128            441             98
        0              0              1


        2              6              6
    21)42           47)282         28)168
      42             282            168
       0               0              0
```

Pg. 79

```
        8              6            4r 51
    43)344          78)468         96)435
      344            468            384
        0              0             51


        4              5            7r 26
    63)252          63)315         78)572
      252            315            546
        0              0             26


        7            2r 11            7
    92)644          51)113         92)644
      644            102            644
        0             11              0


        5            5r 15            6
    28)140          41)220         73)438
      140            205            438
        0             15              0
```

100

Pg. 81

```
        4 r 78          6 r 6            9 r 19
83 ) 410         13 ) 84          35 ) 334
     332               78                315
      78                6                 19


        2 r 3            6                7
84 ) 171         82 ) 492         19 ) 133
     168              492               133
       3                0                 0


        7 r 10          8 r 2            3 r 9
26 ) 192         16 ) 130         33 ) 108
     182              128                99
      10                2                 9


        3 r 16          7 r 2            4
91 ) 289         18 ) 128         55 ) 220
     273              126               220
      16                2                 0
```

Made in the USA
Las Vegas, NV
30 November 2023

81838096R00057